COMMUNICATIONS WITH INDIA, CHINA, &c.;

OBSERVATIONS

COMMUNICATIONS WITH INDIA, CHINA, &c.;

OBSERVATIONS

ON

THE PRACTICABILITY AND UTILITY OF OPENING A COMMUNICATION

BETWEEN THE

RED SEA AND THE MEDITERRANEAN

BY A SHIP CANAL

THROUGH THE ISTHMUS OF SUEZ;

WITH AN

OUTLINE MAP OF THE ISTHMUS & LOWER EGYPT,

SHOWING

THE TRACK OF THE ANCIENT AS WELL AS OF THE PROPOSED CANAL;

ALSO

EXTRACTS FROM A MANUSCRIPT MEMOIR OF A SURVEY OF THE ISTHMUS, BY M. LINANT, OF CAIRO, CIVIL ENGINEER AND INSPECTOR GENERAL OF ROADS AND BRIDGES TO HIS HIGHNESS THE PACHA OF EGYPT.

BY ARTHUR ANDERSON

GYAN

ISBN : 978-81-212-1547-3(HB)

First Published, 1843

Published, 2018

Published by

Gyan Publishing House
5, Ansari Road
Daryaganj, New Delhi-110002
Phone: 011-47034999, 9811692060
www.gyanbooks.com
E-mail: books@gyanbooks.com

GYAN

Printed at: G. Print Process, Delhi.

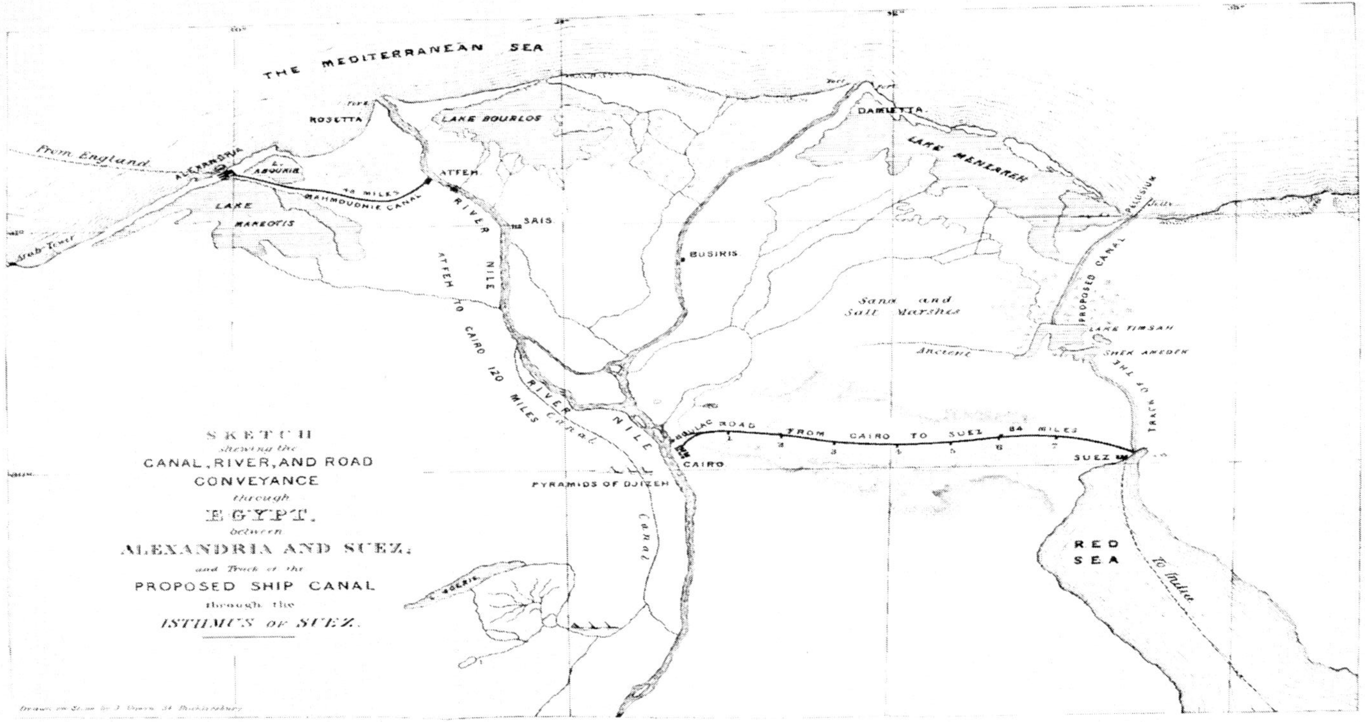
THE MEDITERRANEAN SEA
ROSETTA
LAKE BOURLOS
DAMIETTA
LAKE MENZALEH
From England
ALEXANDRIA
L. ABOUKIR
LAKE
MAREOTIS
48 MILES
MAHMOUDIE CANAL
ATFEH
RIVER NILE
SAIS
ATFEH TO CAIRO 120 MILES
Canal
BUSIRIS
Sand and Salt Marshes
Ancient
PELUSIUM
PROPOSED CANAL
LAKE TIMSAH
SHEK AMEDER
TRACK OF THE
BOULAC ROAD
FROM CAIRO TO SUEZ 84 MILES
CAIRO
SUEZ
PYRAMIDS OF DJIZEH
RED SEA
To India
Arab Tower
SKETCH
shewing the
CANAL, RIVER, AND ROAD
CONVEYANCE
through
EGYPT,
between
ALEXANDRIA AND SUEZ;
and Track of the
PROPOSED SHIP CANAL
through the
ISTHMUS OF SUEZ.

ROUTE OF STEAM SHIPS BETWEEN GREAT BRITAIN AND THE EAST.

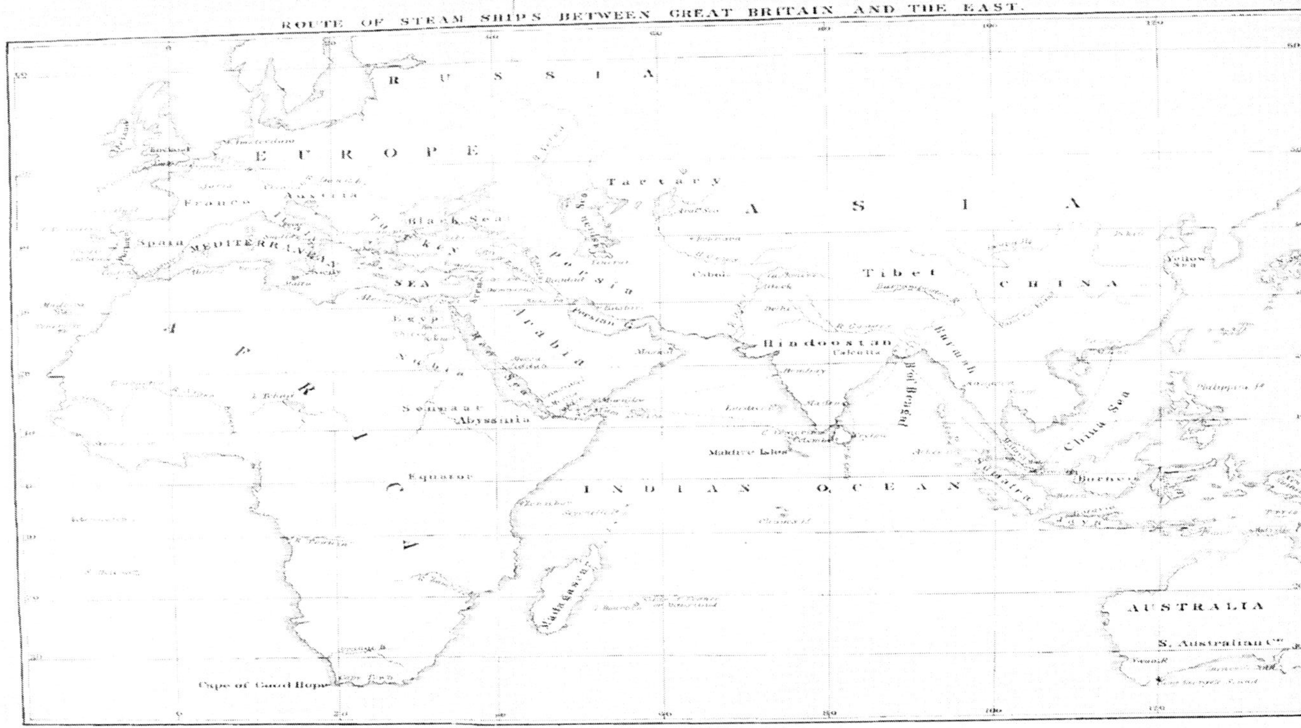

OBSERVATIONS, ETC.

THE interest which has recently been manifested in the improvement of our means of communication with India, China, &c. *via* Egypt and the Red Sea, seems to have revived the speculations, first broached during the occupation of Egypt by the French forces under Napoleon, as to the feasibility of opening a communication between the Red Sea and the Mediterranean by a Canal through the Isthmus of Suez.

Various statements upon this subject have lately appeared in the newspapers and periodicals, both of this country and the continent, and a kind of prospectus proposing the formation of a company to execute the undertaking has just been put in circulation in London.

These statements and speculations, in so far as they have come under the cognizance of the writer of the following pages, are, in a great measure, superficial, crude, or erroneous, * and, therefore, calculated to mislead rather

* Since writing this, an article on the "Suez canal" has appeared in the Foreign and Colonial Quarterly Review, which, although containing some inaccuracies of minor importance, and professing only to take a general view of the subject, the writer would exempt from the above description.

than inform the public in regard to the practicability and utility of an enterprize, whose importance it is scarcely possible to over-rate, considering the nature and magnitude of the interests which would be involved in its successful accomplishment.

The writer has had the means of obtaining information relative to this matter, which he considers may be relied on, and having, in connexion with his duties as a Director of the Peninsular and Oriental Steam Navigation Company, devoted much of his attention to this canal question, he deems the present time opportune for submitting to the public some facts and observations tending, he ventures to believe, to lead to more correct conclusions on this very interesting subject than any which have as yet been published.

These facts and observations will be found arranged under the following heads—

1.—*The physical practicability of the enterprise.*

2.—*The preliminary political arrangements requisite for effecting it.*

3.—*The advantages or disadvantages of navigating by the proposed canal route, as compared with the route by the Cape of Good Hope.*

4.—*Financial considerations.*

5.—*General observations as to the political, commercial, and moral benefits which would be derived from the accomplishment of the undertaking.*

That facility of intercourse creates commerce, and commerce carries with it civilisation, is an axiom founded on universal experience.

Where seeming exceptions to it are found, they may be traced to the blind selfishness of human legislation, counteracting the natural laws established by the all-wise and beneficent governor of the universe.

A project, therefore, which, by severing two continents, proposes to change the whole course of commerce and communication between the eastern and western worlds, and approximate by many thousand miles the knowledge and industry of the west to the ignorance and barbarism of the east, presents considerations of a nature to excite the imagination, and to awaken some of our best feelings in its favor.

In dealing with it, the writer, however, purposes to limit himself to a strictly practical view of the subject. He will state his facts with accuracy—place every circumstance, whether for or against the undertaking, as far as his information enables him to judge, impartially before the reader — and thus leave him to form his own opinion as to the practicability of accomplishing the contemplated enterprise, and of its utility should it be accomplished.

The writer deems it proper to add, that the matter was some time since submitted by him to the consideration of Her Majesty's government, and that the extract from M. Linant's survey of the Isthmus, herein given, appears in the "*Commercial Tariffs, Regulations, &c., of Foreign*

Countries, part 10, *presented to both Houses of Parliament, by command of Her Majesty,* 14*th July,* 1843," being part of those valuable compilations, for which it is well known the country is indebted to the talents and industry of Mr. Macgregor, of the Board of Trade.

PHYSICAL PRACTICABILITY OF THE ENTERPRISE.

The improvement of our communication with the East has been, for some time past, an object of much public solicitude, and in proportion to the progress made in its development its importance becomes more and more manifest. The establishment of a steam communication with India, &c , *viâ* the Mediterranean and the Red Sea; although as yet only in its infancy, has already been productive of considerable benefit, both to Great Britain and her Oriental dependencies.

But, although the steam communication presents a greatly improved means of transit by this route for passengers and letters, it cannot, except in a comparatively very limited degree, be made available for the general purposes of commerce. The transport of all articles of merchandise of moderate value, compared to their bulk or weight, must, from the small stowage-room afforded by steam vessels, and the expense of the transit across Egypt, continue to be effected by means of sailing vessels navigating by the long and circuitous route round the Cape of Good Hope.

The principal object, therefore, of the contemplated canal, would be to open a shorter route between Europe and the East, which could be availed of by sailing, as well as by steam vessels, and thus serve the general purposes of commercial intercourse.

Previously to proceeding to treat of the practicability of

opening such a canal, it may be proper to explain how it has fallen to my lot to deal with this subject:—

In the year 1841, I visited Egypt. While there, my attention was, among other matters, directed to the question which has so frequently been mooted, although never hitherto, I think, satisfactorily treated, viz.: the practicability of re-opening the ancient Canal through the Isthmus of Suez, said to have once joined the Red Sea and the Mediterranean.

In following up this object, I became acquainted with M. Adolphe Linant, of Cairo, a French Civil Engineer, of considerable reputation, and who has been in the employ of the Pacha of Egypt, for I believe, upwards of twenty years.

I found that M. Linant had devoted a great deal of time and labor to the practical investigation of this subject,—had recently completed an elaborate survey of the Isthmus, and was in possession of much detailed information derived from a personal examination of the localities through which the proposed canal would have to be cut. Under certain conditions I induced him to furnish me with a memoir on the subject, accompanied by a manuscript map of his survey of the Isthmus of Suez, and of Lower Egypt, in which the site of the ancient and track of the proposed canal are laid down with great minuteness. In short, the map, now in my possession, which is on a large scale, contains a far more complete view of Lower Egypt than any hitherto executed.

The following extract, translated from M. Linant's memoir or report of survey, together with some remarks of my own, which I shall append to it, will put the reader in possession of all the information which I can supply, in regard to the physical practicability of the object in question.

Translation of an Extract from M. Linant's Report.

(In reading the following a reference to the map is recommended.)

"It is well known by the levellings, which were taken with great care during the occupation of Egypt by the French army, and confirmed by the engineers who have worked at the embankments of the Nile, and also by many repeated observations made during my numerous journeys through the Isthmus of Suez, that the level of the Red Sea is higher than that of the Mediterranean, and that it has, at one time, covered the Isthmus.

"This difference of height is during high water at Suez, 9.907 metres (32 feet) above the low tides (which are scarcely perceptible) of the Mediterranean.

"The topographical position of the place shows, that from the Red Sea to a distance of about 22,000 metres (about 71,500 feet), the spot where the ancient canal was re-dug by Amrou, or where the Canal of the Prince of the Faithful still exists, it is only necessary to dig this canal to a depth of 2.90 metres (8 feet 10 inches), when there would be at once established a current of water towards the Mediterranean; because at the end of this distance you enter the bed of the Bitter Lakes, now dry, which are there about 5 metres (16 feet 4 inches) lower than the Red Sea. From thence the ground becomes lower and lower, as far as the point which separates the Bitter Lakes from the lake *Timsah*, where the ground for a distance of about 6000 metres (about 19,500 feet) is at its greatest elevation, 0.50 (19½ inches) above the level of the sea; the soil is here sandy. Next come the basin of the lakes *Timsah*, much lower than the Red Sea, and which is covered by the waters of the Nile during the inundations.

"The distance between this lake and the low marshy swamps of *El-Karesh* is, at the most, only 3,000 metres (about 9750 feet), and the land is not more than one metre (3 feet 3 inches) higher than the Red Sea; this ground is also sandy.

"Leaving the basins of the lake *Timsah*, and passing behind the hill of *Chek Amedek*, near which the Canal of the Pharaohs, above mentioned, must have passed, we find the ground is nearly every where on a level with the Red Sea as far as *El-Karesh*.

"From thence to near *Das-el-Cassah*, and afterwards in a direction towards *Bir-el-Divietar*, we follow the traces of the ancient canal, in a direct line from one sea to the other, the ground being all sandy and much lower than the Red Sea. From thence to the ground which is inundated during the floods of the Nile, by the waters of the Lake of Manzaleh, there is again found a bed, or sort of excavation, or sandy valley, which may probably have been the ancient canal. From thence to the entrance of Tineh, passing between Faramah and the ruins of Pelusium, the land is 9 metres (29 feet 6 inches) lower than the Red Sea. This line should be followed in opening a communication between the one sea and the other. All this ground having been deposited by the sea, as I shall presently show, it is only necessary to create a current of water in those parts which are not already deep enough in order to cleanse them sufficiently, and get rid of the marine deposits which are formed there.

" The declivity obtained by the difference of level of the two seas, and the body of water employed, would easily form a channel through this soil. A small canal would, in the first instance, alone be requisite to ensure eventually a larger one.

Estimate of the expense of Labour necessary to Cut and Construct the proposed Canal.

STONEWORK.

Piers at Suez, all included .... 1,200,000 piasters.

EXCAVATIONS and EMBANKMENTS.

	Cubic metres under water.	Cubic metres dry.	Labour.	Cost in Piasters.
From Suez to the Bitter Lake, a quarter under water	660,000	....	2,640,000	
At 2 piasters a day, superintendence included	....	1,980,000	2,970,000	
		Total	5,610,000	11,220,000
Between the Bitter Lakes and the Timsah Lakes, earth sandy	....	120,000	240,000	
			Total	480,000
Between the Timsah Lake and El-Karesh, earth sandy	....	120,000	240,000	
			Total	480,000
Dike at Ouadee, 1 man completing 1 metre	....	2,880,000	2,880,000	576,000
Dike at Das-el-Bassah	....	2,880,000	2,880,000	576,000
Dike at Mauzaleh	....	234,000	234,000	468,000
Total of excavations & embankments..........................	....	....	....	13,800,000

" We ought to begin by making at Suez, at the bottom of the port, nearly to where we find the remains of the ancient jetty, made at the entrance of the canal, two embankments or piers, leaving between each an opening which should form the section of the canal to be dug. The canal to be dug to a distance of 22,000 metres (71,500 feet), at a width of 40 metres (130 feet), and at a depth of at least 3 metres (9 feet 9 inches); then to dig from the end of the Bitter Lakes to the lake Timsah* Then to clear out the land between the lake Timsah

* The ground which separates the two lakes.

and El-Karesh, being, as stated before, a distance of 6,000 metres (19,500 feet), leaving only a width of 10 metres (32 feet 6 inches;) this land being sandy towards the west of the lake Timsah, there must be a dike to prevent the waters from spreading over the cultivated lands of Egypt. At the Das-el-Ballah there must be a similar dike, to prevent the waters spreading themselves in the canals of the same name, in the Lake of Manzaleh. Also in the inundated lands about Pelusium and Faramah there must be a dike constructed at the same time, in order to prevent the waters spreading themselves over the lake; the hollow made by forming this dike will form the course of the canal.

" These works being terminated, the canal shut between the two embankments at Suez should be opened with great precaution, only to letting the waters flow in little by little, so that they may take the course intended for them; and, forming their own bed, these waters will pass through 22,000 metres (71,500 feet) of the canal so dug, and will enter the basins of the Bitter Lakes, where the declivity of the waters will give them an impetus or swiftness, that will both deepen and widen the canal, carrying into the basin of the Bitter Lakes the earth and sand of these places; and as the bottom is in some places 16 metres (52 feet) deeper than the Red Sea, there will be no fear that the latter may be filled up. This basin being filled from the sea, the water will flow through the communication established between these basins and the lake Timsah. It will become deeper, as the canal near Suez has deepened of itself. The Timsah lake being full, the waters will flow through the communication dug between this lake and El-Karesh, and at length find their way into the Mediterranean.

" In this manner, by the Ouadee or Manzaleh there is no fear of inundating Egypt; because the waters of the canal, after taking their natural course, will have nearly the same general form as those of the Nile during its inundation; and thus, from the dike at Ouadee, to that of Das-el-Ballah, there will be a rise of only 2 metres (6 feet 6 inches) at the first, and less at the second. At the dike of the Manzaleh they will be at the same elevation as the river at Damietta, where a dike of a metre high is necessary to prevent the waters overflowing the land. At the dike of Ouadee the level of the land is two metres lower than the level of the Red Sea; and in consequence of the inclination of the canal, the water will be 4 metres (13 feet) lower than the water at Suez; thus at Ouadee the land will be 2 metres higher than the waters of the canal, after it has taken its natural course.

" The dimensions of this canal, between the embankments will be—

	metres.		ft.	in.
In length, supposing it to reach to the Mediterranean	180,852	equal to	587,769	0
In breadth, at the surface	50	,,	162	6
Mean breadth	40	,,	130	0
Depth..	9	,,	29	3
Section from where the impetus is	369	,,	11,993	0

"The canal through the lakes and neighbourhood will take the form which the accidental position of the land may give it; but these dimensions will be those requisite for the rise of the water, and the fall will not undergo any material alterations.

"It will be seen that by an outlay of 3,750,000 francs, and by employing paid men instead of soldiers, the work could easily be done.

RECAPITULATION.

Cost of embankments		13,800,000
Cost of works		1,200,000
Total in piasters		15,000,000
In Francs	3,450,000	
	300,000	
		3,750,000 francs
In sterling money		£ 150,000

"In not paying the men, but employing the army, doubling the work as before, it would only require 3,000,000 francs, and 9583 men's labour for 360 days.

"Three objections may be raised to this mode of constructing the canal.

"The first is, that the level of the Red Sea, at the bottom of the Gulf of Suez, being higher than that of the Mediterranean, the phenomenon may be but accidental, and in this case, the communication of the water being free, the level of the Red Sea would be lowered, and the current naturally disappear or diminish, as the canal became filled.

"The second objection is, that the Red Sea being so much higher than the Mediterranean, the water, if it had a free passage, would rush towards the Mediterranean, and would cause a diversion, and destroy the embankments.

"The third is, that on the Egyptian or Pelusian coast, no port or harbour could be formed, and that the Port of Suez being filled with sandbanks, vessels could not be navigated to the canal entrance.

"The primary objection at first seems reasonable enough, but on reflection we see nothing to fear. Throughout the Isthmus of Suez we remark reefs of shells, which are exactly similar to the accretions or collections on the sea-shore; and from which circumstance we should be led to infer that they were deposited by the action of the sea, when there was a communication between Suez and Faramah; but as the like deposits are to be found in the Bitter Lakes, at the level of the Red Sea, and those at El-Karesh, Bir-el-Devietar, and Abou-rok, which are much lower, it seems to prove that such deposits must have come from the lakes, when they were full of water; and also when there existed an artificial communication from one sea to the other; for if this circumstance had arisen from a natural and free communication, these reefs of shells must have followed the inclination or declivity of the Red Sea to the Mediterranean.

"The examination or survey of the land goes to show, that in remote periods, of which no history exists, that there has been a free communication between the two seas. Therefore the question is, what has formed the isthmus, and intercepted the communication? I have carefully examined the ground, and there is nothing to warrant our attributing its formation to the upheaving of the soil between the Red and Mediterranean Seas, nor between Suez and the Bitter Lakes, the only places higher than the Red Sea. It has again been said, that the interruption of the communication between the two seas is caused by the action of the easterly winds filling up the passage, and so forming the isthmus. We have always held very monstrous ideas about the encroachments of these sands, but in reality they are but in a trifling degree of an agressive nature. They could never have had any effect, for if there has been a communication (which appears certain), why has it been filled up? There could have been no powerful current (and one can hardly believe this to have been the case), for wherever traces of like communications are visible, a current is invariably found; and there must have been a more powerful one here, on account of the difference of level, if these two seas have always been in their present condition. But it is to be observed, that in many places the Mediterranean has retired. In the Red Sea, at the bottom of the two gulfs of Suez and Akaba, the contrary has been remarked, especially at Akaba. There are at the latter place the remains of a town, 'Astab,' of which a portion is now under water. Besides, almost everywhere in the winding of the Red Sea, there is visible, at a short distance from the edge of the water, a reef of flat stones, covered with corals, over which flows two metres of water; and under it (the reef being simply a projection) about 10, 19, and 20 metres, with a bottom of sand. This reef of level rocks appears to me to have been the original boundary of the Red Sea. Towards the north there is more water at the present time on this bank than towards the south. One may almost decide that the Red Sea is higher at Suez than nearer the Straits of Babelmandeb; which fact may be explained by the action of the winds from the Indian Ocean, which ingulf the waters in the Red Sea, and cause them to flow towards the north; whilst the winds which prevail at the further end of the gulf, coming from the north-west, do not sweep equally over the whole length of the Red Sea, and therefore cannot counterbalance the action of the wind of the ocean forcing the waters into the gulf.

"The result of the foregoing observations may be as follows:—If the Red Sea be indeed higher at the further end of the Gulf of Suez than it is at Babelmandeb, in opening for it a communication with the Mediterranean, the level will decrease, and, in fact, might become equal to that of the Mediterranean, so that there would be no declivity in the canal of communication between the two seas, which would be a great inconvenience. But if the waters are driven back by the action of the wind to the further end of the gulf, the whole level of the Red Sea will not be higher than that of the Mediterranean. But in order that such a phenomenon might ensue, there should be an equilibrium between the power of the wind which impels the particles of water cast into the end of the gulf, and the pressure of these particles, accumulated at the end of the gulf, and raised to a height of 9.907 where they are higher than the Mediterranean. Without this occurrence the waters of the Red Sea would recover their level in the whole basin as far as the ocean, which is supposed to be at the same level as the Mediterranean; thus an open and unconfined communication being established between the two seas—if the Red Sea descend from the level, the speed would always remain the same, while the preceding calculation proceeds from the height of the Red Sea above the Mediterranean, and that this height of the accumulated waters arises from the impulse given by the winds, which would give the same speed. Therefore, whether the Red Sea may be *entirely* elevated above the level of the Mediterranean, or merely at the end of the gulf, there will be always a speed in the canal equal to that which has been calculated, as arising from the difference of the level of the water at Suez and Pelusium.

"As to the second objection, it has been frequently repeated, and even by persons of talent it has been explained, but without examination.

"As all the rivers which flow into this vast reservoir, (the Mediterranean) carry their waters there, when swelled by winter torrents and melted snow, how could a quantity of water so small, in comparison, as that which would be poured in by the projected canal, cause the slightest difference? In one year this canal would pour into the Mediterranean 8,014,253,140 metres. The surface of the Mediterranean having been computed at 2,459,343,734,475 square inches, it follows that this quantity of water would not cause an elevation of 0.0003 per annum —a mere nothing;—and again, on the supposition that the Mediterranean neither ebbs nor flows, and that the evaporation remains the same with a much larger quantity of water, it is clear that the fears on this ground are quite puerile.

"The third objection—that respecting the port, is more important. It is true that the side of the "embouchure" of the Pelusian Branch has no shelter; and that although the anchorage may be good, nevertheless vessels are not secure; but when the communication canal is open, the alteration of the course of water will force an entrance to the sea for this canal, and minature straits like those of the Dardanelles or Gibraltar may be formed. Even under the most unfavorable circumstances there would be sure to be a passage at least as deep as that of the branch of Damietta or of Rosetta, because the declivity of the canal will be like that of the high Nile, and will continue without change.

"The entrance to the canal will not be encumbered like the mouth of the Nile, for the canal will neither have mud nor weeds; thus in the most unfavorable circumstances we can always count upon having at least 13 feet of water. The boats of the Nile—steamers and vessels of moderate draughts, alone fit for the navigation of the Red Sea, could always enter the canal without anchoring in the bay, and without being obliged to do so. There might be a port in the canal itself—at the lakes of Timsah or El-Karesh. After all, if a port is wanted, it could easily be constructed (the canal being once established), and a stone breakwater might be placed on the self-formed bar which would at once form a protection or shelter for such vessels as might be obliged to anchor going out of the canal. It would cost about 2,500,000 piasters. The sluices placed there to deepen the narrow channel would be useless; for if destroyed, the sand bank which is formed there would be reproduced in the sea, on account of the peculiar formation of the bottom of the sea, and the effect of tides on the Egyptian coasts: for a distance of more than two leagues from the shore the bottom is level, with not above from 15 to 18 feet of water. As to the port at Suez, the deposits being nothing but sand, when the current for the opening of the canal shall be established, those will be easily removed: in case it should be found necessary, at a later period, to dig the narrow channel on account of the tides, a sluice dam, independently of the canal of communication, might be established."

The substance of the preceding extract may be briefly summed up thus:—

1, That the nature of the soil and a chain of lakes present great facilities for excavating a canal through that part of the Isthmus pointed out for its track.

2, That the Red Sea at Suez being higher by 32 feet than the Mediterranean at Pelusium, the water being once let into the canal would form a perpetual current through it, flowing from the Red Sea to the Mediterranean at a velocity of about four miles per hour, and that this stream would not only keep the canal clear, but gradually deepen it; that any apprehension of this opening altering either the level of the Red Sea or the Mediterranean is groundless and puerile.

3, That a Breakwater or Pier might be constructed on the bar which would be naturally formed at the embouchure of the canal in the Mediterranean, in order to form a shelter for vessels anchoring off the entrance of the canal.

4, That the excavation, embankment, and masonry of the

canal, which from sea to sea would be about 100 English miles in length, would require 7,500,000 days labor of one man, or supposing 5000 laborers to be constantly employed, it might be completed in little more than four years.

5, That the cost of excavation, embankments, and masonry, at the current cost of labor in Egypt (about 5d. per day) would be about £150,000
and the cost of a pier or breakwater, at its embouchure in the Mediterranean 25,000

Total.........£175,000

This estimate I consider very far below the outlay which would be required; for two reasons.—1st, Because the section proposed by M. Linant is scarcely of sufficient width, and not a sufficient allowance made for deepening tbe entrance at Suez. 2, Because the cost of erecting the pier or breakwater appears to be considerably under estimated, the shore of the Mediterranean, at that part where it would be required, being so very flat. Neither indeed does it appear that the practicability of constructing such a breakwater and forming a harbour for vessels entering or coming out of the canal has as yet been sufficiently ascertained. It is not, however, necessary at present to discuss at length these points, because should circumstances ever concur to render this enterprise an object of adventure to private capitalists, doubtless a verification of M. Linant's survey and estimates by other engineers, of first-rate eminence, would be an indispensable preliminary to any outlay being made on the works; and if the canal should be found to afford the advantages over the ordinary route by the Cape of Good Hope for sailing vessels, which are hereafter alluded to, it would yield a revenue sufficient to repay an outlay of several millions, as I shall endeavour to show under the head of "Financial considerations."

PRELIMINARY POLITICAL ARRANGEMENTS.

Assuming that the survey and report of M. Linant, in as far as the physical practicability of making the canal and breakwater shall be found correct, the next question for consideration is, what political obstacles may stand in the way of accomplishing the execution of this great work?

The co-operation or, at least, the concurrence of the Pacha of Egypt would be indispensable.

It is true that the Sultan of the Ottoman Empire, as sovereign of the soil, might make a grant of the site of the canal to whomsoever he pleased; but such a grant, without the concurrence of the Pacha, would prove a mere nullity, as he could, if it did not meet his views, thwart and impede the undertaking in an infinite number of ways. It has been recently asserted that the Pacha had granted or was ready to make to a speculator in Egypt a grant for making this canal. But I consider I have good grounds for discrediting such assertion, and that even if the Pacha should be disposed to avail of the assistance of European capitalists in executing it, he would only do so under such an arrangement as would secure to himself the sole right of property in, and control over it.

The making of a canal of communication between the Red Sea and the Mediterranean has been at various times suggested to Mehemet Ali, but as yet he has never been induced to attempt it.

A short time previous to his becoming embroiled in the wars consequent on his differences with the Porte, he commenced a canal which was intended to form a communication from the Nile at the head of the Delta to the Red Sea. The principal object of this canal was however for purposes of irrigation, by conveying the waters of the

Nile over a large tract of desert country and bringing it into cultivation. It would also have served as a passage for small craft between the Nile and the Red Sea.

After an outlay of about equal to £200,000 sterling had been made in labour and material, the work was suddenly abandoned, and has never since been resumed. The exact cause of its being discontinued has not been stated. Some alleged, that the large expence deterred the Pacha from proceeding with it; others, that his resources being absorbed in his warlike operations against the Porte, he had no money to spare for such local improvements. Probably both causes may have contributed to it. This canal, although it would, no doubt, have facilitated, to a considerable degree, the transit of goods, passengers, baggage, &c., through Egypt, would fall infinitely short in general utility of a ship canal directly across the Isthmus, which would admit ships of large tonnage to pass through with their cargoes, and thus save the heavy expense and delay of unloading, transporting across Egypt, and re-shipping.

If Mehemet Ali, after an extensive and somewhat dearly-bought experience, is now rather slow to enter upon any undertaking of magnitude, on the recommendation of European projectors or speculators, it is not to be wondered at; for no man, has perhaps, ever suffered so much from listening to such recommendations His well-known zeal for the introduction into Egypt of European improvements, brought about him a host of schemers and adventurers, who led him into all kinds of experiments, many, or indeed, most of which ended in loss and disappointment.

I consider it doubtful, whether Mehemet Ali will be induced to enter upon such a speculation as the opening of the contemplated canal, except through the intervention of one or more of the European powers, who may have the greatest interest in such an improved means of communication with the East.

It seems probable that he might require a guarantee from these powers that the right to the tolls of the canal should be secured in perpetuity to his family and descendants. Also, that should the tolls at such a rate as might be fixed, and the maximum of which should be regulated by the guaranteeing powers, fail to yield a fair return, (the percentage, of course, to be specified) upon the capital expended on its construction, that these powers should make good the deficiency for a certain term of years.

That there would be little risk of loss under this last condition, provided the construction of the canal upon the scale which I have suggested, should prove practicable, will, I think, be satisfactorily shown, when I come to treat of "Financial Considerations."

But the verification of its physical practicability by parties, whose competence and integrity shall be such as to command implicit confidence, must precede, of course, any political intervention of the nature which I have ventured to suggest.

And it may be a question, not unworthy of the consideration of Her Majesty's Government, whether the comparatively trifling expenditure from the public purse, which would be requisite to obtain, with the concurrence of the Pacha, such a survey as I now hint at, might not be very properly incurred. The surveyors, as I have already observed, should be men of first-rate standing in their profession; and further, I would suggest, that their employment on this survey should render them ineligible to be employed as contractors, or in any other manner in the construction of the canal.

Under such guarantees, and a favorable result of the preliminary investigation, which I have recommended, there would be no difficulty in obtaining the capital requisite for the work, should the Pacha require such aid, which probably he would not, as his average annual revenue is equal to about four millions sterling; and being able, now that he has settled his quarrel with the Porte, to reduce his military establishments, his financial affairs are considered to be in a flourishing condition.

Having suggested the expediency of the interposition of one or more of the European powers to remove any political impediments which might stand in the way of this enterprise, it appears necessary to take a brief view of the interest which they would each have in promoting it.

Great Britain, from the vast extent of her commerce and political connexions with the East, would, undoubtedly, derive the greatest advantage from it; but most of the other nations of Europe would derive benefit in proportion to the extent of their commerce; and those, having ports in the Mediterranean and Levant, or indeed any where nearer to the proposed communication than the ports of Great Britain, would gain more in proportion.

Holland, next to Great Britain, would, from the extent of her trade with the East, have a direct interest in the accomplishment of the proposed enterprise. Her commerce would be improved, and her political connection with her extensive colonies of Java, &c., would be much strengthened by it.

France would derive most important benefits. It would create almost a new commerce for her, in which, through her ports in the Mediterranean, she would have the advantage over us in importing direct, the raw silks, indigo &c., of India, of which, she requires such large quantities for the use of her manufactories, while the shorter route which would be opened to India, &c., would give a stimulous to her exports.

Austria, there is every reason to believe, would give a cordial support to the undertaking. She is making active and judicious efforts to extend and improve her commerce; and there is little doubt of her co-operation in promoting an undertaking so well calculated to further her views in that respect. The merchants of Trieste have been the first to avail themselves of an arrangement which the writer of this succeeded about two years since in effecting with the Pacha of Egypt, by which he agreed to relinquish the high rate of transit duties in Egypt, imposed by the treaties with the Porte, and to substitute so low a rate of duty as would admit of the transit through Egypt of goods to and from India, &c. Under this arrangement, two cargoes of India produce have been already brought from Bengal to Suez in sailing vessels, thence transported across Egypt to Alexandria, whence they were brought to Trieste.

The chamber of commerce of that port are, it is well known, anxious to extend their trade with the East in this direction, and it is stated, that a proposal was, a short time since, made by some Austrian capitalists to the Pacha, for opening a canal through the Isthmus.

Greece would obtain a decided benefit by it. Her numerous small vessels would be well adapted for trading with the ports of Africa and Arabia in the Red Sea, and they would soon be seen covering these coasts.

Italy, Turkey, Spain, Portugal, Belgium, the minor northern states, and even America, would all participate more or less in the improved route for eastern commerce, and, taking a just view of their own interests, would hail it as a benefit.

Even *Russia*, although possessed of an over-land communication with central Asia, India, and China, would gain an advantage by the canal, as she could open a maritime intercourse with the east through her ports in the Black Sea, which would be less costly, and susceptible of greater extension than a land transit.

It hence appears, that all the European powers would have an interest, more or less, in promoting this enterprise; and there appears to be reasonable grounds for concluding, that if requested by one or more of the first-rate powers, either to undertake the work himself, or permit it to be undertaken by private capitalists, under such an arrangement as would connect his name with it, and secure to himself and his descendants a pecuniary benefit from it, as already suggested, Mehemet Ali would be induced to co-operate in it.

The guardianship of such a passage between Europe and the East, would serve to enhance the importance of his political position, and to strengthen those relations of mutual interest between the ruler of Egypt, and the communities of Europe, which would form the most efficacious guarantee for the continuance of the government of Egypt in the family of Mehemet Ali.

The association of his name with so magnificent an enterprise, would, I consider, be another powerful motive to a man so ardently embued with the love of fame.

Should a firman or other formal act from the Sultan of the Ottoman Empire, in his character of sovereign of the soil, be deemed requisite for securing a permanent and indisputable right to make and keep open the canal, I should suggest that point being left to the management of the Pacha, who, I have some reason to think, would obtain it much more easily and promptly than if it were attempted through the medium of European diplomacy.

ADVANTAGES OR DISADVANTAGES OF NAVIGATING BY THE CANAL ROUTE, AS COMPARED WITH THE ROUTE BY THE CAPE OF GOOD HOPE.

Before entering on a comparison of these two routes with regard to their navigation by sailing vessels, it may be well to consider what advantages the contemplated canal would afford in facilitating the steam communication with the East, *viâ* Egypt and the Red Sea, commonly, though very erroneously, denominated " the Overland Route."

In order to make this properly understood, it will be necessary to give a brief account of the present arrangements for the transit through Egypt of the mails, passengers, and packages, to and from India, China, &c.

It is, no doubt, generally known, that this communication is carried on by the steamers of the Peninsular and Oriental Company, which ply monthly between Southampton and Alexandria, touching at Gibraltar and Malta, and by smaller steamers belonging to the East India Company, which ply monthly between Bombay and Suez, chiefly for the purpose of conveying the mails. The Peninsular and Oriental Company have now also placed two steam ships, the "Hindostan, and the "Bentinck," of 1800 tons, and 520 horse power each, to ply between Suez and Calcutta, touching at Aden, Ceylon, and Madras. The vessels of the Peninsular and Oriental Company, both on this side of Egypt, as well as on the other side, convey goods, as well as passengers, and the mails; but the East India Company's vessels plying between Suez and Bombay, do not receive goods, and have but limited, and comparatively inferior accommodations, for passengers.

The mails, passengers, and packages, are, of course, disembarked from the steamers coming from England, at Alexandria, and are re-embarked at Suez, in the steamers proceeding to India, on the outward route, and *vice versa* on the homeward route.

It now remains to show, how their transit across Egypt, between Alexandria on the Mediterranean, and Suez on the Red Sea, is effected, with the present cost of it, in order to estimate how far it would be improved by the contemplated canal communication.

The present route across Egypt for passengers and packages, to and from India, may be divided into three stages, in each of which the mode of travelling is different.

1.—Between Alexandria and Atfeh on the Nile, by the

Alexandrian, or Mahmoudié canal, a distance of 48 English miles. This stage is effected usually in about seven hours, in commodiously fitted-up passage boats, drawn by a steam tug-boat.

2.—Between Atfeh and Cairo, by the Nile, a distance of 120 miles. This stage is performed in swift and commodious steam packets, of which there are four belonging to the Peninsular and Oriental Company, and the Egyptian Transit Company. The passage up the Nile, from Atfeh to Boulac, the port of Cairo, is generally made in sixteen to twenty hours, and down the Nile, from Boulac to Atfeh, in ten to twelve hours.

3.—The third, and by far the most expensive stage, is across the desert, between Cairo and Suez, a distance of 84 miles. This has been hitherto looked upon, and, until lately, certainly was the most uncomfortable part of the journey; but since it has been taken in hand by the Egyptian Transit Company, in conjunction with means furnished by the Peninsular and Oriental Company, it has been greatly improved, and the following graphic description given in the Asiatic Journal, by a gentleman from India, who very recently travelled it, will give a better idea of it than any dry detail.

It must be premised, that the hotel accommodation and fare at Suez, of which so uninviting a description is given at the outset, is about to be improved, as the Pacha has in progress there, a hotel and transit depôt on a magnificent scale.

"At Suez we were not long in swallowing a breakfast at the hotel, (*lucus a non lucendo*)—a breakfast in which coarse and bitter bread was fitly accompanied by coffee boiled in brackish water. Immediately afterwards—our baggage having meanwhile been landed, weighed, and sent forward to Cairo on camels—we prepared to cross the desert. The uninitiated reader will doubtless picture to himself a complete Oriental *cortège*, such as we find in the illustrations of the works of Buckingham and Burckhardt—turbaned travellers, long strings of camels, rude tents, guards bristling with arms, a flaring sun, drought, privation, a single palm tree, and the apex of a pyramid in the distance. Ah, *nous avons changé tout cela!* Thanks to the exertions of the British agents and associations, who make it their business to promote the intercourse with India, there is little difference now between travelling seventy miles over a post-road in England and going over the same space of ground on the Isthmus of Suez. Forty vans, each drawn by four good horses, and driven by an Egyptian Jehu, carrying from four to six inside, and none out, transport the living contents of two crowded steamers across the arid and desolate plain which divides Cairo from the Red Sea. Some of the vans have arched roofs, like those of common waggons, waterproof and painted green. They are all light, but very strong, and capable of bearing, without damage, the violent collisions with lumps of stone and rock to which they are exposed in some parts of the road.* The passengers sit, omnibus-fashion, at the sides of the vehicles, entering at the back, an arrangement that is unavoidable from the height of the wheels, (a single pair,) which reach half-way up the body of the van. The seats are carpeted, and the whole thing is roomy and commodious. At the end of every ten or twelve miles, horses are changed at a sort of road-side stable inn, erected for the purpose; at two or three of which the traveller will get a capital dinner, or breakfast, or luncheon, of eggs, mutton-chops, roast pigeons, stewed fowls, potatoes, bread, and good bottled ale, with tea or coffee if he prefer them. Midway, and again at the halting-place twenty miles from Cairo, there are divans or sofas all round the chief apartment, and bed-rooms for ladies and married people. At one of these it is as well to sleep for a few hours, for sixteen hours' continual travelling in the vans will be found *de trop* by people unaccustomed to fatigue. From all this it is obvious that the day has gone by for grand desert, or, as they call it, overland preparations. Let the traveller from India, or *vice versâ*, therefore, shun the tempting advertisements of outfitters as he would a pestilence, and distrust the hand-books and guides as entirely as he would a matrimonial advertisement. All the urgent recommendations that people should provide themselves with camel-saddles, canteens, bottles of water, parasols, braces of pistols, green veils, carpets, &c., are, like the last comedy at the Haymarket, mere *Moonshine*. Dress yourself lightly for the day, carrying a cloak or great-coat for the night. Put a tooth-brush, a clean shirt, and a couple of dollars into your pocket, and you are completely equipped for the trip.

"After the desert—the scenery of which may be described as a dreary flat, only diversified by sand-hills, stones, rat-holes, camel skeletons, and two trees—the view of Cairo, the "City of the Tombs," is extremely pleasing. The Nile meandering through fields of corn or rich pasture land—the white sails of the boats gliding on the river's bosom—the foliage of the gardens in the suburbs of the town—

* These impediments are now in course of removal by order of the Pasha.

the mosques and minarets, the palaces, and the distant, though apparently proximate, pyramids—form a picture grateful to the eye, and agreeable from historical association.

"We dismounted at the 'Great Eastern Hotel,' the head quarters of the Egyptian Transit Company. Two-thirds of the passengers remained at this hotel, the remainder betaking themselves to 'Colombe's Hôtel de l'Europe.' The latter is on every account to be preferred by future travellers. The rooms are cleaner and more spacious—the table is more sumptuously provided—the attendance infinitely better. The charges are, in the aggregate, the same at both hotels. Fifty piastres (the piastre is 2½*d.*) per diem including breakfast, luncheon, dinner, tea, and bed, with *café noir* in the morning. Candles are charged ten piastres, and five (a shilling) are included in the bill for porterage. The wines are good, of their kind, and not very expensive. Marsala, the best and most commonly drank, costs fifteen piastres per bottle, claret thirty piastres, champagne fifty piastres: bottled ale (Bass's and Hodgson's) is drank at ten piastres the bottle.

"The opportunity for sight-seeing in Cairo varies with the arrival of the steamer which is to carry the traveller the *other* half of his trip. If you leave England in the *Oriental* or *Great Liverpool* (having paid your passage "right through" to India,) and find on your arrival at Alexandria that the steamer from India *awaits you* on the other side of the isthmus, the time allowed you by the Transit Company for running about is limited to the few hours which the camel will occupy in carrying your baggage across the strip of desert in anticipation of your journey in the Cairo mail-coach; and *vice versâ,* on your reaching Suez from India, the English steamer being in waiting at Alexandria. On the other hand, if, as was the good fortune of the passengers by the *Hindostan,* on the occasion of the trip now in course of description, you are some days in Egypt in advance of the relay steamer, you may visit the Pyramids, the Pacha's palace at the citadel, and his gardens at Shoubra, the petrified forest, the slave market, the mosque of Sultan Hassan, the mint, manufactories, chicken ovens, &c.—at a cost of fifteen piastres per diem, the donkey which bears you and the *bakshish* to the guides included. A journey to the pyramids is particularly good fun, apart from the antiquarian enthusiasm which a man insensibly *gets up* on these occasions. The ride thither occu-occupies two hours and a half, and should you fortunately be in Egypt while the corn is growing, the scene of your journey is particularly cheerful. Every inch of the ground to within two or three hundred yards of the base of the pyramid of Cheops at Djeeza is cultivated. The perfume of the crisp fresh air is delicious; the lark rises from beneath your feet, the grasshopper (the locust?) disports across your path. As you approach the pyramid, Arab cultivators are seen running from different quarters of the field to offer you their services as guides to the summit.

From the foregoing, it will be seen, that the route across the desert has lost all that danger and privation with which it has been so much the custom to invest it. I can, in a great degree, corroborate the above description of it, for I crossed it twice, at a time when the arrangements and appliances were very inferior indeed to what they are now; only four small and indifferent vans, or rather carts, could then be sported for a party of fifty, twelve of them ladies. Donkey chairs, saddle donkeys, and a few very so-so Arab horses, were the means of travelling used by the majority, and we were something more than two days and nights on the road, or rather in the wilderness. Yet very few complained, or indeed suffered any privation worth complaining about. An unclouded sky, a delicious freshness in the air, which invigorates the frame, exhilarates the spirits, and sharpens the appetite, so predisposes for enjoyment, that fatigue or discomfort, which, in other places and circumstances, would be felt severely, are here but little perceived.

The charge for the transit of passengers across Egypt, as recently announced by the Egyptian Transit Company, is as under:—

FROM ALEXANDRIA TO SUEZ, *or vice versa.*

First Class Passengers each	£15	0	0
Children under ten years, and Maid Servants..	10	0	0
Second Class	8	0	0

With the usual allowance of baggage, which is a camel load for first class, and half a camel load for children, servants, and second class passengers. Extra luggage is charged for at the rate of 16s. per cwt. over and above the foregoing transit rates. These rates do not include wine, spirits, and beer, nor hotel expences at Suez, Cairo, and Alexandria. The Peninsular and Oriental Company have had to pay the above rates of transit to the Transit Company for the passengers recently booked through and through by them, to or from England and India, and for the use of their steamers, passage boats, &c. on the Nile and Canal of Alexandria, are allowed by the Transit Company £3 for first, and £1 : 10 for second class passengers, showing that the chief expense, say £12, is for the transit across the desert.

Allowing for wine, beer, extra luggage, hotel and incidental expenses, it may be fairly estimated that the transit expenses across Egypt of every first class passenger amount to very little short of £20.

When a monthly communication by steam navigation to and from Bengal, Madras, and Ceylon, as well as with Bombay, shall have been established, and towards which a rapid progress is making, it will, I think, be no exaggeration to estimate the number of passengers annually crossing through Egypt to and from India, China, &c. at two thousand. The expense, therefore, of the transit of passengers, exclusive of goods and parcels, will then amount to about £40,000 per annum.

The Indian mails are taken charge of on their debarkation at Alexandria, and until their arrival there from India, by the agents and officers of the East India Company. The steam vessels on the Nile and Alexandrian Canal are not availed of for the transit of the mails, which are conveyed overland between Alexandria and Cairo on the backs of donkeys, each donkey carrying two boxes of letters. Between Cairo and Suez, across the desert, dromedaries are employed. The average of one monthly mail somewhat exceeds one hundred boxes each way, being upwards of two hundred crossing Egypt to and from India, and containing about one hundred thousand covers.

The expense of the mail transit, according to accounts laid before Parliament by the East India Company, amounts to rather upwards of £9,000 per annum.

Taking the transit of passengers at . .	£40,000
The Mails, as at present, at	9,000
And of goods and parcels at say	1,000
It follows that a sum of	£50,000

per annum would be available from steam navigation traffic alone, to be applied, if necessary, as a revenue in remuneration for the capital which might be expended upon the proposed canal, as I shall treat of more particularly under the head of "Financial Considerations."

The transit of the mails and passengers across Egypt, under the present arrangements, occupies THREE days. By the proposed canal it would be done in *one* day from the Mediterranean to the Red Sea, and in *half* a day from the Red Sea to the Mediterranean; a saving of time of no mean importance, and which can scarcely fail to be appreciated in connexion with the question of the acceleration of the mail communication with India, China, &c., now exciting so much public attention.

The exemption of passengers, in their transit through Egypt, from the least fatigue or annoyance of any description—the transit of goods, parcels, specie, &c., without liability to the damage or risk of land and river transit, and frequent change of conveyance—the entire avoidance of contact in seasons of plague—are all most important advantages, which the canal would afford, as compared with the present means and mode of transit. Another, although of a private nature, is of considerable consequence, namely, the being able to have all the steam vessels at home for occasional repair and overhaul.

I shall now proceed to consider what advantages the canal would present to sailing vessels navigating between Europe and the East.

The distance from the English Channel to Calcutta, *via* the Cape of Good Hope, by the route taken by the best

sailing vessels, may be put down at	13,000	miles.
Viâ the Mediterranean, the Red Sea, and Indian Ocean, it is about	8,000	
Gain in distance by the latter route, to or from Calcutta	5,000	miles.

By the Cape route to Bombay it is about ..	11,500	miles.
By the Red Sea route	6,200	
Gain in distance to or from Bombay ..	5,300	miles.

This is, of course, assuming the navigation by the Mediterranean and Red Sea route to be of equal facility with the Cape route. And I shall now endeavour to examine this part of the question with the accuracy which its importance demands.

The first point which presents itself in this consideration is the influence of the monsoons, or periodical winds, which prevail throughout the Indian Seas, and in the southern part of the Red Sea.

The S. W. monsoon, which blows much stronger than the N. E. monsoon, prevails in the Indian Ocean, between the east coast of Africa and the coasts of India, &c., from May until October, blowing with the greatest force during the months of June, July, and August.

The N. E. monsoon prevails from October to May, but is of much less force than the S. W. monsoon.

In order to estimate the difficulties or advantages of these periodical winds, to a sailing vessel navigating by the Red Sea, as compared with the route by the Cape of Good Hope, we must, for vessels bound to or from the most important commercial ports in India—the Presidencies of Madras and Bengal, as also Ceylon, Sincapore, Java, China, &c., suppose her placed at a point a few degrees to the southward of

Ceylon from or to which she would have to proceed whether navigating by the Cape of Good Hope, or by the Red Sea route.

Now, it is well known, that from this position a vessel steering for the coast of Africa towards Cape Guardafui (the southern extremity of the Gulf of Aden), and thence to the Straits of Bab-el-mandeb (the entrance of the Red Sea) would carry the wind a-beam, and could therefore make her passage to or from the Straits of Bab-el-mandeb, and the given point to the southward of Ceylon, during the whole of the south west monsoon.

As the N. E. monsoon blows in an exactly opposite direction to the S. W. monsoon, and is much more moderate, a sailing vessel could make good her course between the Red Sea and the same point south of Ceylon, equally well as in the S. W. monsoon, and therefore during the whole year could effect this part of the passage with tolerable certainty.

Vessels proceeding to or from Bombay would have to arrange their passages to suit the monsoons. Sailing from England, or other places in Europe, so as to have the S. W. monsoon in their favor; and sailing from Bombay for Europe so as to have the N. E. monsoon in their favor.

It hence appears that the monsoons present no particular difficulties in the voyage between India, &c. and the entrance of the Red Sea, more than in the ordinary route by the Cape of Good Hope; but that, on the contrary, for ships trading with the eastern and most important parts of Hindostan, and to Ceylon, Malacca, Singapore, Java, China, &c. this part of the voyage would be made with more certainty than an equal distance in the Indian Ocean, of a voyage by the Cape of Good Hope route.

The Red Sea Passage.

The length of the Red Sea from the Straits of Bab-el-mandeb to Suez is 1200 miles, its medium breadth about 150 miles, and its direction nearly N. N. W. and S. S. E.

Its coasts on either side are fringed with coral rocks, which render it dangerous in navigating it to approach near its shores.

In the southern part of it, say from the latitude of Jidda to Bab-el-mandeb, being about one-half of its whole length, the southerly monsoon predominates nearly two-thirds of the year, commencing in October and ending in May or June. The northerly winds then set in, and continue about four months, say June, July, August, and September.

Outside the Red Sea, in the Gulf of Aden, the wind generally prevails from the eastward for six months, say from October to May, and from the westward during the other part of the year.

In the northern part of the sea, from Jidda to Suez, but more particularly near to Suez, the prevailing winds for nine months of the year are northerly, and in the months of June, July, and August, it is very difficult for sailing vessels to beat up to Suez. In this part of the Red Sea southerly breezes are at all times, but of short duration.

The best time for vessels to sail from Suez for India, &c. is therefore about the end of August, which will enable them to clear the Straits of Bab-el-mandeb in September, before the easterly winds commence in the Gulf outside.

From all these facts it will appear,

1st.—That the passage between India, &c., and the Gulf of Aden, may be made with ordinary facility by sailing vessels.

2nd.—That some delay would be experienced by sailing vessels in the Gulf of Aden during certain portions of the year, whether bound to or from India; and also by vessels *coming from India,* in the northern part of the Red Sea, during the greater part of the year.

Against these difficulties in the Red Sea route must, however, be set off the delays by calms and contrary winds, between the trades experienced by vessels navigating by the Cape route. In order to ascertain how nearly they may balance each other, and consequently whether a saving of time in navigating by the Mediterranean and Red Sea, proportionate to the shorter distance, as compared with the voyage round the Cape of Good Hope, might be effected, I would beg leave to submit the following questions to the consideration of experienced nautical men.

1st.—Is the navigation by a sailing vessel, between England and Pelusium, say 3000 miles, of equal facility as a similar distance from England on the Cape route?

2nd.—Is the navigation to or from the given point, to the southward of Ceylon and Cape Guardafui, more certain than that of an equal distance between the same point and the Cape of Good Hope?

3rd.—Would the impediments in the navigation of the Red Sea and Gulf of Aden, already pointed out, be greater or less than those experienced from calms and contrary winds between the trades in navigating by the Cape of Good Hope route? And, assuming that the answer to the second query should be in favour of the Red Sea route, would that gain set-off against the difficulties of navigating the Red Sea and Gulf of Aden, reduce the latter to a par with the impediments between the trades just alluded to?

4th.—Would not the nature of the coast of Egypt, at the embouchure of the Canal in the Mediterranean, present considerable difficulty and danger to sailing vessels approaching it for the purpose of seeking tbe Canal entrance? The coast, it is well known, for a distance of upwards of 150 miles to the eastward, as well as to the westward of the

Canal entrance, is destitute of any sheltered anchorage—is exceedingly low, and not easily discoverable until within a short distance of it, and very shallow at a distance of two leagues from the shore. A good light on the Pier or Breakwater might obviate some of the danger, but still it is to be apprehended, that sailing vessels approaching this part of the coast, with the wind strong from the North and N.W., and which is very prevalent, would incur considerable risk of getting embayed and being driven ashore.

If the result of this investigation should be such as to place the difficulties and facilities of each route on a par, it will then follow that a gain in time of from four to six weeks would be effected in navigating to or from India, &c. by the proposed canal, as compared with the Cape of Good Hope route.

Before concluding this part of the subject, I think it well to advert to another objection which may possibly be raised against the canal passage, namely:—The difficulty of tracking a vessel of heavy burthen through the canal, from the Mediterranean to the Red Sea, against a current of three to four miles an hour, which would be the velocity of the stream constantly flowing from the Red Sea to the Mediterranean.

To this may be answered, that the same northerly winds which prevail as already stated, for the greater part of the year, in the upper or northern part of the Red Sea, also blow across the Isthmus, and consequently the vessel would be for the most part able to stem the current by using her sails. In default of this a sufficient number of dromedaries would track a vessel of almost any size, or posts placed along the banks of the canal for warping would effect the object on occasions, which would be of but rare occurrence, of a failure of wind.

It is to be considered also, that as the beds of the Bitter

Lakes and of the Lake Timsah, would form two very extensive basins in the course of the canal, nearly half-way between the Mediterranean and the Red Sea, these would become halting places or inland ports, and here steam tugs would no doubt, among other accessories, be found, should the canal ever become a general channel of intercourse.

From the Red Sea *to* the Mediterranean the vessel would, of course, be carried along by the stream.

FINANCIAL CONSIDERATIONS.

Although from the political and commercial importance of this undertaking, assuming its practicability to be established, it would be money well laid out even by Great Britain alone, to expend a million for opening the canal; I shall consider it merely in the character of a commercial enterprise, dependent for its being undertaken on its capability of yielding an adequate return for the outlay required for its execution.

To ascertain this the value of the existing trade between Europe and the East; the amount of tonnage required for its transport; the advantages afforded by the canal route as compared with the Cape of Good Hope route for sailing vessels navigating to and from India, China, &c.; and the probable extension of the intercourse with the East by steam navigation, must all be kept in view.

TRADE BETWEEN EUROPE AND INDIA, CHINA, ETC.

The amount of maritime trade with British India, and other places in the East, is stated to be as follows:—

Total Exports of merchandize and treasure from
Bengal, Madras, and Bombay, to Great

Britain, Continental Europe, and America, annually	£12,000,000
Total imports to ditto from ditto, annual average..............................	8,000,000
Trade of Sincapore and China, Java, &c.	6,000,000
Annual value of trade with places to the eastward of Egypt	£26,000,000

Tonnage of Vessels trading between Europe and the East.

The amount of tonnage of *British Shipping only*, which entered inwards and cleared outwards at British Ports, from and to places within the limits of the East India Company's charter, in the year 1841, was, according to a published statement of the East India and China Association,

	727,587 tons,
Of this, the tonnage of ships to and from the Cape of Good Hope and South Sea Fishery, which would probably not avail of the canal route, and is therefore deducted, was	30,309 „
Remains (British tonnage)	697,278
Add tonnage of shipping trading to and from Batavia, and the Dutch settlements in the East, estimated in round numbers at	200,000 „
Total British and Dutch	897,278 ..

Taking into account the tonnage of French and other European flags trading with the East, and keeping in view the increased stimulus which has of late been given to the development of the resources of British India; the improved commercial relations on the point of establishment between Europe and the vast and populous empire of China, and the new sources of trade which the canal communication would tend to open up with Arabia, Abyssinia, &c. through the Red Sea, I think I shall not be considered as making an exaggerated estimate in putting down the shipping which will be trading between Europe and the East, about the time when the canal might be expected to be opened, at one million of tons.

It now remains to estimate from the forgoing *data* what sum might be obtained from this trade as a revenue for the proposed canal,

Assuming that sailing vessels would gain four or five weeks on a voyage to or from India by the canal, and that goods could be placed in the respective markets in so much shorter time than by the Cape route, a saving of interest on the investment to the merchants would be effected, and although this is only one of many other advantages which a diminution of the time of transit would yield; I shall only take it into my estimate as being the most tangible, and the least liable to dispute.

Taking the average rate of interest at five per cent. (it is much higher in India, and somewhat lower in England) the saving on the whole trade between Europe and the East would be, say on £26,000,000 — about one per cent., or £260,000.

I will, however, only estimate this saving on the finer articles of the trade, such as indigo, silks, &c. from the East, and the finer articles of European produce and manufacture exported thither, which authentic *data* will bear me out in estimating at £10,000,000 sterling. One per cent. upon this would amount to £100,000. I will, however, only estimate it as paying the present reduced transit duty of half per cent. established by the Pacha, at the instance

of the Oriental Steam Navigation Company, or..	£50,000
Two dollars, or say 8s. per ton, would not, I think, be objected to by vessels using the canal, as a toll, considering that for this they would save upwards of a month's wages, provisions, wear and tear, &c., besides obtaining a higher rate of freight than vessels navigating by the Cape or long route. And for this toll I will only estimate one-fourth part of the shipping trading to or from the East, say 250,000 tons, at 8s.	100,000
Revenue on merchandise and shipping	£150,000
Add contributions from passengers, parcel and mail transit, as estimated at p. 29.	50,000
Annual revenue	£200,000

Equal to a dividend of five per cent. on a capital of four million sterling.

I will now, however, take a view of the financial prospects of the undertaking, under different circumstances from those just assumed, by supposing the difficulties of navigation or otherwise to be such as to afford no inducement for sailing-vessels to prefer the canal route to that by the Cape of Good Hope; and that, consequently, the only traffic from which a revenue could be derived, would be that carried on by steam navigation in passengers and freight, and the transit of the mail communications.

As already shown, this latter traffic and transit might contribute (without reckoning on the extension, of which I shall presently show it to be susceptible) to the extent of £50,000 per annum, which of itself would yield a return of five per cent. on one million, being nearly six times the capital estimated by M. Linant.

There is, however, another circumstance which, although I have not as yet alluded to it, may, I think, without impropriety, be brought forward, inasmuch as it will tend still more strongly to show, that even putting altogether out of the question the navigation of the canal by sailing vessels, there are still sources of remuneration to the Pacha, available as a sufficient guarantee for a fair return on the probable outlay, either to himself or to any private capitalists who might undertake the enterprise.

A few months since, I was commissioned by the Pacha to make on his behalf a communication of a confidential nature to Sir Robert Peel. I availed myself of the occasion to press upon the Premier's attention, the disadvantages to which our important mail communications with India, China, &c. were liable to be exposed from the present footing on which their transit through Egypt rested, namely, in a great measure on the mere goodwill and gratuitous protection of Mehemet Ali. And I ventured at the same time to suggest the expediency of Her Majesty's Government adopting some steps to effect such an arrangement with the present Pacha, as should secure the permanency of the transit through Egypt of these communications, and be binding, not only on the Pacha, but on his successors in the government of Egypt, and thus ensure the safe transit of the communications, or give us a just right of interposition in the case of any circumstance arising to cause their interruption.

Subsequently the matter has been pressed upon the attention of Government by means of memorials from the leading merchants of London, Edinburgh, &c. and others connected with India, and is now, I have reason to believe, under the serious consideration of the proper department.

The basis of this arrangement I suggested to be the payment to the Pacha of a certain annual sum in lieu of transit postage, he undertaking, in consideration thereof, to find the means for the transit across Egypt of the mails, to guarantee their safety, and their transit within a given time, from sea to sea.

It is, perhaps, not unreasonable to assume, that some such arrangement may ere long be concluded, not alone by this government, but by some other of the European powers, in proportion to the extent of their communications with the East; and that these compositions for transit postage may amount to a considerable sum, say £20,000 to £30,000 per annum. At 6d. per letter (about the rate of *reduced* transit postage which we now pay to France under the last postage convention) the correspondence now passing through Egypt, which amounts to something upwards of one million of *covers*, would give at least £25,000.

The suggested arrangement with the Pacha might, I think, be made subservient to induce him to undertake or co-operate in the making of the canal, inasmuch as this might be made one of the conditions of the transit convention. The sum to be allowed to him for transit postage, together with that which it has already been shown could be contributed by the traffick in passengers and parcels, would form a sufficient guarantee for an adequate return on the capital which would probably be required to complete the work, if it should be found at all practicable, as the two sums together, would, in every probability, somewhat exceed £60,000 per annum.

But when we consider the vast field for commercial operations with Europe, now on the point of development in the East; the improvements in steam navigation now in progress, tending to economise the consumption of fuel, and to afford greater space for the stowage of cargo—together with the important facilities which the Canal passage would afford for the improvement and extension of steam communication between the eastern and western worlds, it will scarcely, I think, be deemed a visionary anticipation, to predict, that in the course of no very distant period, steam navigation, with such facilities, would become the medium of transmission, not only for letters and passengers, but for a large proportion of the finer articles of commerce, and would, consequently, be capable of contributing a revenue for the support of the Canal, if needful, much beyond the sum which I have herein estimated. It therefore follows, that an adequate return on the probable outlay would be obtained from steam navigation traffick alone, and that consequently the practicability, for sailing vessels, of the Canal and Red Sea route, is not a question which ought alone to determine the expediency, or otherwise, of attempting the enterprise.

GENERAL OBSERVATIONS AS TO THE POLITICAL, COMMERCIAL, AND MORAL BENEFITS WHICH WOULD BE DERIVED FROM THE ACCOMPLISHMENT OF THE UNDERTAKING.

In a political point of view, the facilities which the Canal passage combined with steam navigation, would afford to Great Britain, as regards the government of her Indian empire and dependencies, are almost incalculable.

From Malta troops could be placed in Bombay in *three weeks*; in Ceylon and Madras in four weeks; and in Calcutta in five weeks. And by means of the frequent intermediate coast communication in India, which the extended and comprehensive plan of steam navigation anticipated to result from the opening of the Canal passage would afford, troops and stores could be rapidly moved from one station to another.

Let any military man compare this with the present mode of effecting similar operations. The long sea voyage by the Cape of Good Hope, of four or five months, in a sailing vessel. The men worn out, and requiring almost as many months more after debarkation, to recruit their health and strength, so as to be fit for active duty: the length of time, and great fatigue, in moving between distant military stations—and I think he will admit, that India might, with the facility alluded to, be efficiently governed with one-half the number of European troops which is now required. The facility for despatching ships of war, and stores of all kinds, to or from India, &c., need only be glanced at to be at once appreciated. The stability of British power in India would be thus increased, while the cost of maintaining it would be considerably diminished.

To estimate the importance of the proposed communication in a commercial point of view, it is necessary to take into consideration the extent of the field of operations for commerce, which the vast and populous regions of the East present. India contains one hundred millions of subjects of the British crown, and there are fifty millions of adjacent tributaries and allies; in all, one hundred and fifty millions in the Peninsula of Hindostan, exclusive of the island of Ceylon. Little has as yet been done to stimulate the people to improve their resources and ameliorate their condition and habits; but of late years more attention has been directed to these objects, and the trade with British India has been rapidly on the increase.

China contains, it is estimated, not less than three hundred and fifty millions of inhabitants, said to be inclined to industry, and to be peculiarly addicted to traffic. A timid and jealous system of government has for ages hermetically sealed, as it were, this vast country and population from intercourse with the rest of the world. British valour has now removed the barrier and opened this almost new world to European commerce.

Let us suppose that the people of India and China should, from improved intercourse, require to the extent of one shilling per annum, for each individual, in value of British manufacture or produce. Even this seemingly insignificant amount would produce an annual increase of twenty-five millions in our exports. The opening of the canal route would tend greatly to facilitate our intercourse with the five-hundred million of people who inhabit India and China, and hence its commercial importance must be sufficiently obvious.

The application of steam power to the purposes of navigation, is doubtless one of those mechanical discoveries destined to effect a great moral revolution in the human mind throughout the world. The printing press has contributed, in an immense degree, to the progress of civilisation, by furnishing a means for the spread of thought. But it seems scarcely to admit of a question, that the power of steam, applied to navigation, will exercise a more extensive, a more rapid, and a more efficacious influence in accelerating the civilisation of the world than even the printing press.

I have observed at the outset, that facility of intercourse is commerce, and commerce is civilisation. The accomplishment of the enterprise in question would very essentially facilitate the intercourse between Europe and the five hundred millions of human beings inhabiting Hindostan and China, who remain to this day enslaved by debasing superstitions, and sunk in mental darkness and delusion. What a field is here opening to the christian philanthropist! To aid in the removal of ignorance and superstition by the diffusion of useful knowledge, and an enlightened religion; to plant industry and the arts where indolence and barbarism have hitherto prevailed, are noble efforts, tending no less to elevate those who engage in them, than the objects of their exertions. The opening of the proposed communication would obviously subserve the promotion of such objects, and therefore can scarcely fail to excite an interest in the mind of every sincere well-wisher to his fellow creatures.

The preceding statement and observations will, I trust, be sufficient to show that the object of which they treat is, at least, of sufficient importance to warrant an effort being made to ascertain, in the manner suggested, whether it be practicable or not, and if found practicable, whether, and in what manner, the Pacha of Egypt would be disposed to concur or co-operate in it. If the information and suggestions therein given should lead to such a result, the chief object of their publication will be attained.

APPENDIX.

HISTORICAL RECORDS OF THE ANCIENT CANAL OF COMMUNICATION BETWEEN THE RED SEA AND THE MEDITERRANEAN.

Although in the preceding pages I have limited myself to a mere practical view of the subject under existing circumstances, it may not be uninteresting to many readers, to have before them a brief analysis of the testimony, found in ancient writers, of the former existence of a canal of communication between the Red Sea and the Mediterranean.

Nearly the whole of the ancient authors, who have written on Egyptian history, speak of this communication. But the most explicit is Diodorus Siculus, (Book I. sec. 1,) who says, "*A canal of communication has been made from the Gulf of Pelusium to the Red Sea. Necos, the son of Psamaticus, commenced it. Darius, King of Persia, continued the work, but afterwards abandoned it, under the advice of some engineers, who told him, that by opening it he would inundate Egypt, which they had found to be lower than the Red Sea. Ptolemy II., however, did not hesitate to achieve the enterprise; but he caused to be placed, in the most convenient part of the canal, barriers or dams, very ingeniously constructed, which were opened when ships wished to pass, and were afterwards quickly closed,*" &c.

It is stated subsequently, that Cleopatra would not permit her vessels to pass from the Mediterranean into the Red Sea across the Isthmus, which clearly implies that there must either have still existed a canal, or at least traces of it, or traditions of the fact, the time not being very distant from that of Ptolemy II., who accomplished the work.

Herodotus, Strabo, and various other ancient writers may be quoted in confirmation of the testimony of Diodorus; but as the curious in this antiquarian branch of the subject can easily refer to the books themselves, it seems unnecessary to enlarge upon it by further quotations.

After the period above referred to, the canal appears to have been suffered to fall into decay, and little or nothing is heard of it until comparatively modern times. Immediately after the establishment of Mahomedanism, Amrou attempted to re-establish the communication from Faramah to Suez, which the Caliph Omar, in A.D. 644, completed; and the navigation between the Red Sea and the Mediterranean, by this canal and the Nile, remained open about 120 years, when it was blocked up by the Caliph Motassem to prevent Christian vessels proceeding to the ports of Arabia, and it has never since been re-opened.

These records, and the traces of the canal still remaining, as described in the report of M. Linant, scarcely leave a doubt of its former existence, and consequently of the practicability of re-opening it, especially when the superiority of modern over ancient engineering skill is taken into consideration.

RAILWAY ACROSS THE DESERT OF SUEZ.

Mehemet Ali has at various times had it in contemplation to make a railway between Cairo and Suez. Some years ago he even had a considerable quantity of iron rail brought from

England for the purpose, part of which he afterwards used for his stone quarries, and the remainder has lain useless on his hands ever since. This project seems to have been very recently revived. Late advices from Egypt state that the Pacha had actually contracted with a party in Egypt for the supply of the rails, but that in a day or two afterwards the contract was annuled,

A railway across the desert is a project which I consider would be subject to two important disadvantages. Its utility would not be very great, and it consequently would present but little means of yielding an adequate return for the outlay in constructing it. Out of the 250 miles distance from Alexandria to Suez, or from sea to sea in crossing Egypt, the railway would afford an improved means of transit for 84 miles only. Passengers to or from India (forming almost the entire traffic) now perform this stage of the route as already shown, in carriages with tolerable comfort, in about 16 hours. By a railroad they would do it in four or five hours, Would the difference be worth any considerable enhancement of expence? And if not, how is a sufficient revenue to repay this outlay to be obtained from a comparatively small number of travellers passing through Egypt once a month or so?

With regard to goods, a camel carrying, if required, 400 lb. weight, can be hired for the trip between Suez and Cairo, for thirty to forty piastres—six to eight shillings. A rate any thing near this would afford no great remuneration for a railway, and any thing much higher would operate as a bar to goods in any quantity passing by this route, in preference to the Cape of Good Hope route, even if steam navigation admitted of its transport, which at present it does not, except to a very inconsiderable extent. The transport of both goods and passengers by the Nile and canal would remain as before; and as regards goods, would be attended with all the inconvenience, risk, and expense of landing, loading, re-loading, river and canal risk, and re-shipping, as at present. The facilities which would be obtained for the general interests of commerce and intercourse by a railway appear therefore to bear no comparison with those which would be obtained from a canal, while the expense of the former would probably exceed that of the latter.